WYANDANCH PUBLIC LIBRARY

D0855977

Wyandanch Public Library
Wyandanch, New York 11798

LET'S VISIT BELIZE

Let's visit
BELIZE

TRICIA HAYNES

ACKNOWLEDGEMENTS

The Author and Publishers are grateful to the following organizations and individuals for permission to reproduce copyright illustrations in this book:

S. C. Bisserot/Nature Photographers; Anne Bolt; A. J. Cleave/Nature Photographers; The Greg Evans Photo Library; Government Information Service, Belize; James Hancock/Nature Photographers; Michael Holford; Impact Photos; Jim Long/TRIP; David Oliver/TRIP; Royal Commonwealth Society; Voluntary Service Overseas.

© Tricia Haynes 1988

All rights reserved. No reproduction, copy or transmission of this publication may be made without written permission.

No paragraph of this publication may be reproduced, copied or transmitted save with written permission or in accordance with the provisions of the Copyright Act 1956 (as amended), or under the terms of any licence permitting limited copying issued by the Copyright Licensing Agency, 7 Ridgemount Street, London WC1E 7AE.

Any person who does any unauthorized act in relation to this publication may be liable to criminal prosecution and civil claims for damages.

First published 1988

Published by
MACMILLAN PUBLISHERS LTD
Houndmills, Basingstoke, Hampshire RG21 2XS
and London
Companies and representatives
throughout the world

Designed and produced by Burke Publishing Company Limited
Pegasus House, 116-120 Golden Lane
London EC1Y 0TL, England.

Printed in Hong Kong

British Library Cataloguing in Publication Data
Haynes, Tricia
Let's visit Belize.—(Let's visit).
1.   Belize—Social life and customs—
Juvenile literature
I.   Title
972.82'053   F1443.8
ISBN 0-333-45522-3

Contents

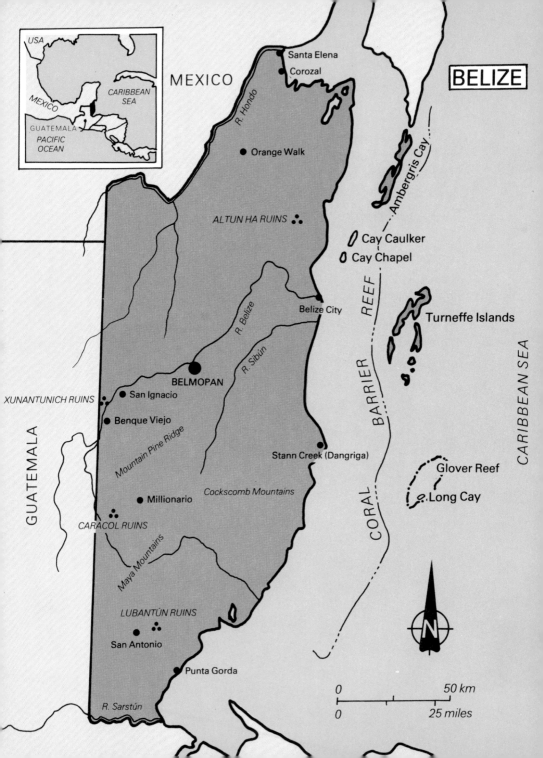

The Land and Its People

Belize is a tropical country in Central America. It is some 280 kilometres (174 miles) long and 109 kilometres (68 miles) wide and covers an area of 22,965 square kilometres (8,867 square miles). On the north and northwest it is bordered by Mexico, on the south and west by Guatemala, and on the east side by the Caribbean Sea. Off the coastline lie small islands and cays (islets), some of which are inhabited. Belize's Coral Barrier Reef runs the length of its coastline and is the longest in the world after Australia's Great Barrier Reef. The country's beaches, with their white coral sand fringed by palm trees, are among the finest in the Caribbean.

Belize was formerly ruled by the British and used to be known as British Honduras. The first Britons to settle in the country in the seventeenth century were pirates who had ventured into the region and decided to stay. They established settlements, despite the fact that the coastal areas of what is now Belize were thought to be inhospitable. Next came Scottish

7

A roseate spoonbill. These birds inhabit the swamps of Belize and feed by sieving the mud through their spoon-shaped bills

woodcutters who also claimed the territory. The land proved to be ideal for them as there was an abundance of logwood.

Since 1973, the country has been called Belize. The name was taken from Belize City, the former capital, and is thought to be derived from the name of a pirate called Wallis who was one of the first British settlers to make his home there during the seventeenth century. Another theory is that the name is actually derived from the Maya Indian word *beliz,* meaning "muddy waters".

Most of Belize is low-lying and swampy. The country is divided into three principal regions. The northern part, where the Hondo River forms a border with the Yucatan (a region of Mexico), is a low-lying area with lagoons and marshes

8

which attract many wildfowl. Belize has some of the largest concentrations of waterbirds in Central America. As the land in the north of the country is flat, it is ideal for the growing of sugar-cane.

The Maya mountain range lies in the central and south-western region. This chain of mountains rises in parts to over 900 metres (3,000 feet) above sea level. Savanna land (open grassland with scattered bushes and trees) is found on the western edges of the Maya mountains. The Cockscomb range lies to the north of the Maya mountains, the highest peak being Cockscomb at 1,122 metres (3,681 feet). From north to south run coastal plains, much of which comprise swampy ground formed from alluvial deposits. Mountain Pine Ridge, a range of low mountains between Cockscomb and the Guatemalan frontier, is now a national forest reserve with extensive pine forests, ancient Maya Indian ruins, underground caves and cataracts.

The north and coastal areas are swampy, with mangroves growing in abundance, while around the mountain chains in the central regions is agricultural land.

The chief rivers of Belize are the Hondo River in the north; the River Belize, which flows through the centre of the country from Belize City to the town of San Ignacio on the Guatemalan border; the Sibún River, which rises in the mountains and flows into the Caribbean not far from Belize City; and the Sarstún River in the south. All four rivers are fast-flowing, and small boats can navigate them for most of their course.

An evening scene by a canal in Belize City. The many canals and the river contribute to the high humidity level

As Belize lies in a tropical zone, the climate is hot and humid. However, the sticky heat is moderated by the trade winds which blow from the northeast and·make the stiflingly hot months of May to October bearable. The temperatures vary depending upon the seasons and altitudes, with a low of 21 degrees Celsius (70 degrees Fahrenheit) and a high of 35 degrees Celsius (95 degrees Fahrenheit). Usually the temperature fluctuates between 25 and 30 degrees Celsius (77 and 86 degrees Fahrenheit), although on occasions night temperatures drop to 16 degrees Celsius (60 degrees Fahrenheit).

Belize has two main seasons—the rainy season from May to October, and the dry season between November and April. In both seasons, the humidity is intense and can reach ninety per cent in some inland areas. The rainfall is high, with an average for the country as a whole of 2,000 millimetres (80 inches) a year. In the north, the average annual rainfall is 1,270 millimetres (50 inches), while in the south it is 4,300 millimetres (170 inches). As a result of the heavy rainfall, vegetation in Belize reaches immense proportions.

Because Belize has an abundance of forests, wood provides a good source of income. There are several different kinds of timber, including mahogany, cedarwood, rosewood and, in the hilly regions, pitchpine. Due to the tropical climate all kinds of crops—including bananas, oranges and lemons, sugar-cane and oil palms—can be grown. Rice, manioc, cocoa, cotton and exotic fruits such as mangoes are also found. Like other Central

Canoes such as this one travel up the rivers of Belize as well as plying between ships in Belize Port

American countries, Belize has a variety of brightly-coloured flowers such as wild orchids.

There are over five hundred species of birds and many types of animal. The dense forests give shelter to peccaries, deer ocelots and jaguars, as well as the small native animal, the gibnut, a kind of dormouse. Marshes and swamps provide homes for ducks, quail and numerous waterbirds. In the waters of the Coral Barrier Reef, an immense variety of fish and crustaceans can be found.

After El Salvador, Belize is the smallest of the seven countries which make up Central America. It is one of the least densely populated countries with approximately 158,000 inhabitants

One of the many beautiful flowers growing wild in Belize

A peccary, native to Belize

and only fifteen people to the square kilometre (thirty-nine people to the square mile). The people of Belize come from a variety of racial backgrounds and include black Caribs, Maya Indians, *mestizos* (people of mixed American Indian and Spanish descent), and Creoles (locally born descendants of European settlers), with a small percentage of Europeans.

British pirates who settled in Belize brought with them black slaves from the West Indies. These were the Garifuna, or black Caribs, who were a mix of African slaves and American Indians. Gradually, these people intermingled with the people of Belize. The black Caribs maintain their traditions and each year celebrate their ancestors' arrival in the country.

Maya Indians crossed into Belize from the Yucatan in

13

neighbouring Mexico, and their Spanish-speaking descendants now farm the land. Many of them now live in the northern areas of Orange Walk and Corozal on the Hondo River, where sugar-cane is their principal crop. *Mestizos* (people of mixed American Indian and Spanish blood) crossed the border from Guatemala to settle in Belize where taxes were lower. Jamaicans, Germans and Italians also arrived; and later came Arabs, chiefly from the Lebanon; and some Chinese. A small number of British families, chiefly Scots, remain. Thus Belize today is a home for several ethnic groups and nationalities.

Most Belizeans are Christians. Half the population is Catholic, but there are many Anglican churches, as well as other Protestant denominations such as Methodists, Mormons and Evangelicals.

The official language of the country is English, but Spanish is also widely spoken, with at least one-third of the population being native Spanish speakers. However, the language most often heard is *patua* (patois)—a mixture of English, French and black Carib, with American Indian and Spanish words thrown in, and spoken in the lilting tones of Caribbean island people.

The official public holidays in Belize are New Year's Day, Baron Bliss Day on March 9th (commemorating a British settler), Labour Day (May 1st), National Day (September 10th), Columbus Day (October 12th) and Carib Settlement (or Garifuna) Day on November 19th. Christmas is also celebrated.

Unlike other Central American countries, Belize has few folk traditions. About fifteen per cent of the population are

14

A man tussling with a bullock during a rodeo—a form of entertainment which is often a feature of public holidays

descended from Maya Indians. This group is aware of its traditions and is proud of its heritage. The Maya maintain their link with the past by speaking Indian dialects. The black Caribs have maintained some of their traditional ceremonies and enthusiastically celebrate their arrival in Belize on Garifuna, or Carib Settlement Day every year. Their national festival centres on Stann Creek (also known as Dangriga), a town with a true black Carib atmosphere. For the most part, however, the varied nationalities of Belize seem to have forgotten about celebrating ethnic ceremonies. Apart from honouring local saints, there are nowhere near the number of fiestas that are seen in the rest of Latin America.

Visitors can travel to Belize by air, sea or road. Belize

These American Indian schoolgirls are direct descendants of the Maya. They wear traditional beads with their uniforms

international airport lies about 16 kilometres (10 miles) north-west of Belize City. Regular services operate from the U.S.A., Guatemala, Honduras and El Salvador.

The long stretch of coral reef makes it difficult for ships to approach the Belize coastline, but small boats come in from Florida and New Orleans in the U.S.A. Some ships also ply between Belize City and Puerto Cortes in Honduras.

By road Belize can be reached from Mexico and from Guatemala City which connects with the Pan-American Highway. However, Belize's roads are the worst in Central

16

America and this makes the journeys long and arduous. Most roads are unpaved and many are flooded during the rainy season, so four-wheel-drive vehicles are often used.

Much of Belize has remained undeveloped, its jungles and forests isolated, thus giving it the appearance of an empty, almost uninhabited land of little value. It has few industries and needs much financial aid, but its past shows a civilization of amazing sophistication. The builders of that civilization were the race known as the Maya.

Maya Territory

Many centuries ago, much of the territory of modern Belize was inhabited by a race known as the Maya. It formed part of an empire which also included present-day Mexico, Guatemala, El Salvador and Honduras. Between the third and ninth centuries A.D., the Maya built pyramids, temples, ball courts and plazas where they worshipped their gods and lived an organized, disciplined life.

In the northern part of Belize, 53 kilometres (33 miles) from modern Belize City, they built the city of Altun Ha ("Water of the Rock"). There they established temples. Their temples were a splendid sight, with carved altars, standing stones and images of the Maya Sun God. They also used Altun Ha as a trading centre. It was close to both the sea and the Belize River. This enabled the Maya to trade their jade, shells, vases and carvings with people from both neighbouring inland places and overseas. The Maya of Altun Ha probably traded with those of Tikal, a vast and imposing city in neighbouring Guatemala.

These are jade *flares* found in Belize. They were once suspended on wire and worn as earrings by the Maya

On the Guatemalan frontier, about 128 kilometres (80 miles) southwest of Belize City, the Maya set up another great city known as Xunantunich, ("Maiden of the Rock"). They built their fabulous city, which possessed elaborately constructed buildings and temples, on the top of a hill so that they could survey the surrounding territory. One of the pyramids, El Castillo, rose to 40 metres (130 feet), giving excellent views over Belize and Guatemala. Even to this day, El Castillo remains the tallest building in Belize.

Like their neighbours in Altun Ha, the Maya of Xunantunich quickly established centres trading with both the cities of the coast and those hidden deep in the jungle. Xunantunich became one of the chief Maya cities of Belize and flourished until the disappearance of the Maya during the tenth century.

From these two important bases the Maya spread out across the country establishing their cities. In the foothills of Mountain Pine Ridge they built Caracol; and, farther south in the Maya mountains, near the town of San Antonio, Lubantún. From there they had easy access to Punta Gorda on the Caribbean coast. When Lubantún was excavated, it was discovered that the Maya had used no mortar to hold their stones together. Subsequent excavations unearthed giant standing stones, some reaching nine metres (thirty feet) high.

At El Pozito, near August Pine Ridge, structures dating from

Mayan ruins at Xunantunich

around A.D. 250-450 have been excavated, including the pyramid which formed the centre of the Maya city.

In the northern part of Belize, close to Orange Walk, another Maya site known as Lamanai has been excavated, revealing a ceremonial altar and artefacts. But most amazing of all is the excavation at Cuello, near Orange Walk, which has revealed one of the earliest architectural structures in the Maya world, dating back to around the third century A.D. In the same region, the earliest examples of Maya craftsmanship were found—namely ceramic objects dating from the third century A.D. Up to that time, the colours used to decorate pottery had been mainly browns and dark reds. The Maya invented new colours with which to decorate their objects, and the objects found in the Cuello region show clearly that they used at least six colours in their decorations. They also proved themselves skilful draughtsmen and designers. The objects which have been found show that, although they did not have gold to work (as did the Maya of Guatemala and El Salvador), they were highly artistic in the fields of pottery and design. How far they travelled is an open question, but it is clear they were not only cultivators of land, great architects and designers but also good tradesmen, exchanging the objects they produced with people from both neighbouring areas and overseas. It is likely that they had contact with the Maya of Guatemala, Mexico and El Salvador while maintaining their own lifestyle in Belize.

As yet, much of the Maya territory in Belize, with its fabulous cities and temples, is still overgrown or buried by the ever-encroaching jungle. Little trace of their civilization now remains, except for the few objects which have been recovered from cities like Altun Ha and Xunantunich and are now on show in Belize's museums. We do know, however, that the Maya empire and its people extended right across Belize and that the Maya easily outnumbered today's sparse population— some archaeologists estimate by as much as tenfold. We can only hope that with fresh excavations new discoveries about the Maya people will be made.

Following the disappearance of the Maya, Belize's history was uneventful until the first Europeans arrived in the country during the sixteenth century. The Spaniards had come to South America in search of gold. They assumed that all Central America, including Belize, would also be full of gold and precious objects such as they had found during their conquests of Panama and other countries. However, they quickly reached the conclusion that Belize had neither gold nor even minerals which they could use. Furthermore, the territory was inhospitable, consisting of disease-ridden swamps and impenetrable jungles. The Spaniards soon abandoned it.

A century later, British pirates patrolling the territory realized that they could use the bays and hidden coves to lure ships onto the rocks so that they could loot the vessels and off-load their cargo. Although the terrain was difficult and the reefs dangerous to shipping, the pirates established bases in Belize and its cays. The pirate Peter Wallis, who settled in one of the bays in 1638, is the man after whom Belize is supposedly

Typical examples of Mayan stone carving

named—although some people hold the contrary view that the country's name is derived from the Maya Indian word *beliz*.

The pirates were followed by their compatriots who left the British Isles having heard of the abundance of timber in Belize. They set themselves up as woodcutters, for the jungles which covered the country clearly showed that the timber trade would be a highly profitable one.

With the growing demand for mahogany in Britain, the British woodcutters (most of whom came from Scotland) soon had more work than they could do alone. Many of them brought in black slaves from the Caribbean islands to help them; and in a short time black Caribs outnumbered the British settlers. Trade was brisk and profitable. Soon the impenetrable forests of Belize were being cut down and the wood shipped to

23

Foresters dragging mahogany tree-trunks out of the forest. Timber, once moved laboriously by slaves, is now carried by trucks

England where famous furniture-makers such as Hepplewhite and Chippendale fashioned the wood into chairs, tables and cabinets. The stately homes of England were soon overflowing with expensive furniture, while the woodcutters far away in Belize endured a hard life working in the forests and disease-ridden swamps.

The Spaniards, who had previously shown no interest in the territory, now realized that large sums of money could be made from log cutting. They decided to attack the British settlements in an attempt to drive out the British so they could take over the lucrative wood trade. But, despite their efforts, they were finally obliged to withdraw. The British, who now considered themselves Belizeans, returned to their business and their profits.

Business was booming. Cargo ships plied back and forth, setting out from Belize laden with logwood. But by the late eighteenth century Spain had decided that Belize was too profitable to be allowed to slip from its grasp. The Spaniards tried every way they knew to win back Belize, especially by government pressure. At last, a treaty was secured whereby it was agreed that the British could go on cutting and exporting logs providing the land was not used for agricultural purposes. The British, who were making such good profits from the timber trade, had no choice but to agree. However, the treaty was later to have serious repercussions—as no agriculture was permitted, Belize had to import all its food from abroad and thus never established an agricultural base such as most countries need in order to support their people.

Despite the treaty, the Spaniards persisted in their demands. However, at the Battle of St. George's Cay in 1798, the Belizeans won a victory over the Spaniards, defeating an army of 2,500 men together with thirty Spanish ships. Today, the Belizeans celebrate the victory each year on National Day, September 10th.

The British Presence

Between the sixteenth and eighteenth centuries, Spain had come to control a number of countries in South and Central America. In the early nineteenth century, these countries struggled to win their independence. Mexico and Guatemala gained their independence in 1821, and both countries then claimed possession of Belize. Although these claims were rejected, Guatemala continued to press for possession. An agreement was signed in 1859 in which Guatemala relinquished its claim to Belize on condition that Great Britain built a road from Guatemala City to Belize. However, as the road was never built, Guatemala still feels justified in its claim to Belize.

In 1860 Guatemala threatened to annex the country by military force; and, in view of that threat, Great Britain continued to maintain troops in Belize as few Belizean citizens wished to place themselves under Guatemalan jurisdiction.

In 1862, Belize was declared a British Crown Colony. This

meant that Belize was under British rule, governed from England, but with a governor in Belize answerable to the British Crown. The colony was known as British Honduras—a title which it kept until 1973. At this stage the economy of the country was dependent on timber-cutting and there was little thought of developing it in other directions.

In 1964, in a further attempt to solve the political problems with Guatemala, Great Britain granted rights of self-government to Belize. This meant that the day-to-day running of the country was in the hands of the Belizeans themselves but that Britain still had overall control. The Belizeans, however, were aware of the constant threat of Guatemalan interference and were uneasy at the prospect of standing alone. As a result, when Belize became an independent country in September 1981, it chose to remain within the Commonwealth with the

A typical colonial house with its airy verandahs—a far cry from the meagre houses of the majority of Belizeans

The flag of the independent nation of Belize. The emblems are a reminder of the importance of timber and shipping in Belize's past

British Queen, Elizabeth II, as Head of State. The Queen is represented by a governor who, although he has only limited powers, has at his disposal British army, naval and air force units so that he may protect and guard the frontiers of Belize as set out in the 1859 treaty.

However, Guatemala has always kept a keen eye on events within Belize. And it is not surprising that Belizean citizens feel that, given the opportunity, Guatemala could substantiate its former claims. It is a close neighbour of Belize and has never totally accepted British rule.

In the meantime, Belizeans live and work in a country which, due to British rule in the past, models its political system to a large extent on that of the United Kingdom. The Belizean parliament consists of two political bodies—the Chamber of Representatives, with eighteen members, and the Senate, with eight members. The members of both houses of parliament are appointed by the governor. The parliament is presided over by the prime minister, and it is also his job to maintain contacts with other countries. The seat of government is Belmopan, although the commercial and economic centre of the country is Belize City.

There are only two political parties in Belize. These are the People's United Party, with twelve seats in parliament, which has held power ever since internal self-government was granted and whose leader is the prime minister, and the United Democratic Party, with six seats.

Unlike the neighbouring countries of Guatemala and El Salvador, both of which have experienced guerilla warfare in opposition to the official government, there is no political turmoil in Belize and the country is run on peaceable lines.

Belize is an unspoilt country, with magnificent coral reefs, sheltered cays, a remarkable number of limestone caves and the impressive stone cities of the ancient Maya. Its jungles remain largely unpenetrated, and its swamps still harbour scores of malarial mosquitoes. Belize's roads are in poor condition and are frequently impassable during the rainy season when oceans of mud make travelling hazardous, if not impossible. As a result, the country has remained cut off and isolated from its neighbours. In fact, Belize might have slumbered through the centuries had it not been for the discovery of oil which attracted multi-national companies to the region in the 1970s. However, Belize has produced only slight "shows" of oil, and no strikes have yet proved big enough for commercial companies to exploit. Tourism, too, which is a big money-spinner for many other Latin American countries, is still in its infancy in Belize, with only fifty-five thousand visitors per year.

The small population and poor standard of living offer few opportunities for importers. The people of Belize are remarkably friendly but until recently have had little thought in their heads for industrial or agricultural expansion. For many years they depended on the British to ship in food and raw materials while they dealt with the timber forests. As a result, it never crossed their minds that their country was lagging behind other

A car and passenger ferry. In the rainy season the river will flood and make this route impassable

Belizean women on their way to market. Most of what they buy is locally grown or locally produced

developing nations. When independence came it was small wonder that the Belizeans, for the first time in their history, began to give serious thought to the cultivation of land and to improving their stagnant economy.

The Economy

Aware of the country's dependence on food imports in the past, Belize's government has, over the last few years, attempted to expand agriculture. Although much of Belize's food is still imported, Belizeans are beginning to realize the importance of farming. To this end, large tracts of land are being cultivated, producing fresh fruit and vegetables for the domestic market.

A grapefruit-crusher in operation in a factory in southern Belize

Tending beehives

Belize's economy today is primarily agricultural, with sugar being the most important crop. Vast areas of land in the areas of Corozal and Orange Walk are given over to sugar production. The second most important crop is bananas. Belize's hot and humid climate makes it ideal for fruit-growing, so the southern regions concentrate on citrus fruit production. Tropical fruits such as mangoes are also doing well as there is an increasing demand for them in world markets. Belize's tobacco plantations, though so far on a small scale, are beginning to flourish too. The country is also producing honey and chicle (which is used to make chewing gum).

Little by little, Belize is learning to be self-supporting. Rice-

Spraying young cocoa plants. Cocoa is one of the crops which contributes to Belize's export trade

growing has been one important area of development. Rice is grown both for domestic markets and for export, principally to the U.S.A. Market gardening is also increasing, alongside cocoa and tobacco production. So far, these products have made only a small contribution to the export markets, but it is hoped that the situation will soon improve.

Fisheries will have to be further developed. Belize is fortunate in having a Caribbean seaboard in which all kinds of marine life, particularly shellfish, flourish. In the cays, particularly Ambergris Cay and Cay Caulker, fishermen's co-operatives have exploited Belize's conch and lobster, most of which are exported to the U.S.A. Fish and crustaceans are already the second largest export earner after sugar.

Belize is lucky in having an abundance of timber and, although many of its forests have been cut down, wood is still available in plentiful quantities. Mahogany is much sought after, as are rosewood and cedarwood. Forestry is one area of the economy which Belize can easily expand.

Livestock farming is also gradually being extended, with cattle doing well. In the western regions of Belize, this project is well under way. Pigs are also being reared, and poultry farms have been set up. This, too, is an area where development could be significant.

Belize is slowly proving itself, showing that it will not be the "undiscovered" country of Central America for much longer. It is a member of CARICOM (the Caribbean Common Market), and so has access to both Caribbean and Central American markets. It is also a member of the Caribbean Development Bank, the World Bank and the International Monetary Fund.

So far, there is little industry in the country. It looks as if this will take longer to develop than Belize's agriculture, as there is a severe lack of skills and only a very small local market to cater for, and to draw from. A number of new projects are being considered and the government is constantly looking at the new incentive programmes, which are often put forward by foreign companies.

At present, industry in Belize manufactures clothing, cigarettes, flour, fertilizers and beer. Although oil prospecting was eagerly taken up when the first discoveries of oil were made, the amount produced has been nowhere near as great as anticipated. However, optimism remains high. Tourism is another industry which could be developed but so far little has been done to expand it.

To support its economic policies, Belize has had to take advantage of foreign loans and investments. Some of this money is used to set up incentive programmes. Belize usually has to spend more money on importing goods than it earns

Cutting down a mahogany tree by hand. Nowadays, much of the felling is done mechanically

Cattle-raising in Belize. This type of farming is proving to be very profitable and has considerable potential

from exports because it is not yet able to produce all the foodstuffs and manufactured products which it needs. However, there are indications that its textile and clothing industry is developing, and small-scale businesses are beginning to make some progress. Any large profits can be reinvested in agriculture, which is one area in which the country can expand. Fisheries are another good base for expansion, as world markets can never get enough giant shrimps, lobsters and other shellfish. The marketing of fruit and vegetables can also be developed, and it does seem that the Belizeans are finally beginning to move towards self-sufficiency and true independence.

The vast majority of the population work on the land. The

A Belizean woman working in a garment factory

northern part of the country employs many labourers in the sugar-cane fields. In the mid-1970s the price of sugar rose sharply. The sugar-cane growers, most of whom were Spanish-speakers who had emigrated from Mexico, became rich and began to acquire expensive imported cars and television sets. With the ending of the boom, everything levelled out. Now the sugar-cane growers lead a less affluent life, although sugar remains Belize's number one export.

In the south, workers are employed on the citrus fruit farms;

and in the west labourers work in the livestock industry, raising cows, pigs and poultry. Agricultural wages are low, and for many people in Belize (even those with large families) home is no more than a simple shack.

In the coastal regions, life is less crowded and, even if their homes are of the simplest kind, coastal dwellers always have access to the water, the fine white sandy beaches and the offshore islands. They can make a living by fishing, gathering coconuts and doing odd jobs. If tourism were to be developed to its full potential, the coastal areas would expand fast and jobs

Lobsters being processed for export to North America

An aerial view of Belmopan. The houses seen here are mostly the homes of government employees

would be found for many Belizeans who at present are merely eking out a bare existence.

As Belmopan is the administrative capital and seat of government, most of the workers here are civil servants. Others work in shops and offices. However, instead of the Spanish-style colonial houses found in other South and Central American countries, Belmopan has British-style homes and tin-roofed dwellings built on high stilts. Belize often has to contend with floods, and if homes were not built high above the ground they would be swept away. The height also gives the Belizeans fresh air from the trade winds—a welcome relief after the steamy, sticky heat.

In 1961, Hurricane Hattie partly destroyed Belize City, when

40

a three-metre (ten-foot) tidal wave washed many of its buildings into the sea. Belizeans are accustomed to all kinds of natural disasters. As a result, the ramshackle appearance of their former capital and chief port, Belize City, does not unduly alarm them, but the open sewers, which empty their effluent into the canals, are a major problem and health hazard.

As Belize possessed no gold, silver or mineral deposits, for many years prospectors showed little interest in the country. Then, suddenly, during the 1970s, there was talk of oil "shows". This brought a quick reaction from foreign companies which had reason to believe, from geologists' reports, that this small Central American country might be a source of oil wealth. In fact, drilling in Belize did not uncover the major reserves

This school was built in San Pedro on Ambergris Cay after Hurricane Hattie. Like many new buildings in Belize it is specially designed to double as a hurricane shelter

A typical house in Belize. Although small and unimpressive, such houses are usually kept clean and tidy

which the early prospectors had anticipated, and many companies and individuals lost their investment. Yet they are still speculating; not least Guatemala, Belize's close neighbour, which still claims a right to the territory.

Territorial rights continue to be a problem for Belize and, if a major oil strike were made, it is only too likely that Guatemala would press its claim to the land. This is something the Belizeans shrug off, for they are well accustomed to their neighbours making territorial demands.

As long as there are jobs to be done, the Belizeans are

content. It is only when unemployment strikes that poverty begins to bite and the unemployed become anxious when they cannot provide food for their families. Many people in Belize have no choice but to live in shanty towns where sanitation is poor and life is lived in the most basic way. But at long last there is hope that small-scale industries will begin to prosper and agriculture to expand so that Belize can start to have confidence in the future.

Living in Belize

With only fifteen people to the square kilometre (thirty-nine people per square mile), by comparison with some of its neighbours such as El Salvador, Belize is unexplored territory. Yet this small country is a melting-pot for a range of nationalities. Although basically a mixture of black Caribs, Maya Indians, people of mixed Spanish and American Indian descent *(mestizos)*, and Creoles, it is also peopled by Jamaicans and a small number of North Americans. The prospect of oil encouraged a number of foreign companies to go to Belize. As a consequence, travelling through the country one is immediately aware of ethnic differences. Yet the overall effect is harmonious, for each race has settled in its new environment and gets on well with its neighbours.

Religious freedom is practised throughout Belize; there is complete tolerance for a variety of religious groups and for all Christians from Mormons to Episcopalians. Because the country is small, people make a greater effort to get on with each other.

These children typify the racial strains to be found in Belize: a child of Maya Indian origins (left), a girl of mixed Indian and Spanish blood (centre) and a child of black Carib descent (right)

City-dwellers would not change their lifestyle to live in the isolated country areas; but nor would country farmers, busy on their sugar-cane plantation or in the citrus groves of the south, want to exchange their less hectic lifestyle to go to dance halls or cinemas and to keep pace with the noisy nightlife of Belize City.

Coastal dwellers prefer the ocean, and the aquatic life of the Coral Barrier Reef where fish and coral are plentiful. They prefer the coconut palms to the dirt-filled streets of the cities. It is only when there is widespread unemployment that people begin to move to the cities, and then overcrowding results.

In ports like Belize City, where people look for work as dock labourers, the atmosphere is lively and raucous with music blaring out of bars. Rum is cheap and energy is high. The sticky heat makes it difficult to rest, except when the trade winds blow.

On the sugar plantations life is less complicated although equally hard. The workers get very tired, for cutting sugar-cane is a strenuous job, especially in the steamy equatorial temperatures. The sun beats down so it is not surprising the workers are relieved when it is time to go home.

Belize is a tropical country and, to those unaccustomed to the equatorial sun, the heat seems like a furnace. Belize is also a

Fishing boats and yachts moored at Belize Port, reflecting both local industry and one aspect of tourism

Belizean schoolchildren in class

country of massive floods which cause houses to be swept away, leaving a trail of disaster behind them. Hurricanes are another source of worry for Belizeans, often causing widespread damage. For example, when Hurricane Hattie struck in 1961, many inhabitants of Belize City had to be moved to Hattieville, a temporary settlement 24 kilometres (15 miles) away, created for the people the hurricane had made homeless.

Belize is a malarial area and its swamps once spelled disaster for foreigners. Today, the country is considerably healthier, with medical assistance at hand in the cities. The coastal areas are particularly hot, and visitors often find the heat tiring. Drinking water, particularly outside Belmopan, must always be boiled, and fruit and salad thoroughly washed.

Today, ninety per cent of the population of Belize are able to read and write. Great emphasis is put on education and it is this which accounts for the high literacy rate. All children must attend school until their sixteenth year. Primary and secondary school teaching is in English; and, although they come from a wide variety of races and may speak Spanish or *patua* at home, all children do their lessons in this language. In the more remote country areas, some Indian dialects can still be heard. As with religion, Belize adopts a tolerant attitude to language.

Unfortunately, transportation in Belize remains primitive, with many roads in very poor condition. A new northern highway links Belize City to the Yucatan in Mexico; and the road between Belize City and Belmopan has been greatly improved, although it is still subject to flooding during the rainy season. All main towns are connected by road to Belize City. There is also a road from Belize City to Punta Gorda, but as it is not an all-weather road it too is subject to flooding in the rainy season. Other road surfaces, many of them dirt tracks, are not good, and during wet weather they are totally impassable.

Local air services link the main towns and there are regular services to Corozal, Stann Creek (also known as Dangriga), Orange Walk and Ambergris Cay from the airstrip at Belize City's national stadium. In the outlying districts, people have to manage as best they can.

Belize has one radio station — Radio Belize. This is based in Belize City and is government-owned. There is no official television station but Belizeans can tune in to both American and Mexican television channels. Belize has no daily news-papers but it does have a number of weekly publications, all of which carry advertisements in both English and Spanish. There are no trade journals but the Chamber of Commerce publishes a monthly newsletter to assist importers and exporters.

Despite the British presence in Belize over the years, food and drink tend to be much like the food and drink of the rest of Central America, with abundant supplies of tropical fruit juices, soft drinks such as Pepsi and Coca Cola, and locally brewed beer. There is plenty of rum, as well as a fiery sugar-cane brandy known as *aguardiente*.

Tropical fruits form part of the Belizean diet but the staple foods include sweet potatoes, rice dishes and *tortillas* (pancakes made from maize flour). *Tamales* (pancakes made from boiled

The English signs on these shopfronts are a constant reminder of former British involvement in Belize

maize) are also popular, usually filled with meat or vegatables. As fish is plentiful (the coastal areas, especially the cays and islands, have an abundance of shellfish and locally caught fish), it is eaten as often as possible. In addition, German immigrants introduced sausages to Belize, and Creole food is widespread, much of it consisting of dishes made with rice, red meat or chicken, and beans. Gibnut, the small forest animal which lives in Belize, is also served as a delicacy. As for desserts, puddings and cakes made from coconuts are frequently eaten.

Hotel restaurants may offer international dishes, but for most Belizeans low wages dictate their staple diet which usually consists of rice, beans and maize. But, like people of all impoverished nations, Belizean cooks are experts at making do, and the diet is nourishing, supplemented by tropical fruits and nuts.

Most Belizeans enjoy an outdoor life and, with the Coral Barrier Reef extending the length of the country's seaboard, it is not surprising that weekends and holidays find many people at the beaches. Water sports, such as surfing and snorkelling, are popular, as is scuba diving. Because the Blue Hole of Belize, on Half Moon Cay, is full of strange rock formations, many divers find it a challenge and are eager to investigate it. The waters are warm—rarely lower than 26 degrees Celsius (80 degrees Fahrenheit)—and the clarity is excellent, with visibility as far down as 46 metres (150 feet) in some parts.

Fishing is another favourite activity. It is argued that the waters off Belize offer some of the greatest sport fishing in the

Coconuts being husked. Coconuts are frequently used for making puddings in Belize

world, packed as they are with shark, barracuda, kingfish, amberjack, the great tarpon and the many colourful varieties of snapper. For those who prefer river fishing there are plenty of freshwater fish to be caught.

Swimming and boating are two other popular pastimes, since the beaches of Belize are amongst the most beautiful in the Caribbean.

Inland, the limestone caves which dot the countryside provide a glimpse into the ancient Maya world. It is believed

A Red Emperor—one
of the many varieties
of snapper which live
in Belize's coastal
waters

that this ancient people used the extensive system of caves in Belize as underground hide-outs. Wall-paintings and various artefacts have been found there and, like the Maya ruins, the caves are now tourist attractions, particularly for people interested in archaeology.

In the mountain areas, hiking and rock-climbing are popular, and horse-riding is a great favourite. Bird-watching attracts many people who come to identify the five hundred species of birds to be found in Belize. Botanists, biologists, geologists and oceanographers are all interested in Belize, for its flora, fauna and underwater life are abundant.

As for hunting, the jungles and forests are filled with game such as jaguar, wild boar and deer, while the marshes teem with wildfowl. Camping also enjoys its share of popularity both on the coast and in mountain areas. Most campsites are located in beauty spots such as Mountain Pine Ridge, or in the cays where the scuba diving and snorkelling—in the green waters of lagoons protected by the coral reefs—are among the best the Caribbean has to offer.

The outdoor life is a major advantage for the people of Belize. The natural wonders, available to all Belizeans, make life seem more worthwhile when they are working in the sugar-cane fields and small-scale industries. When they have finished work they can always go to the beach or explore the interior with its mountains, jungles and forests.

Belize City

In 1961, Belize City was struck by Hurricane Hattie. The damage was so extensive that, in 1970, it was decided to construct a new modern capital at Belmopan, in a valley beside the Belize River, 80 kilometres (50 miles) to the west. Today Belmopan is Belize's administrative capital and seat of government with about twenty-nine thousand inhabitants. Almost in the centre of the country, the city was created out of the jungle.

Despite continued fears of hurricanes, however, the people of Belize still consider Belize City to be the chief urban centre of the country. Founded in about 1550, Belize City is built on a mangrove swamp, so the weather is always steamy and intensely humid. Nevertheless, the inhabitants think it has more atmosphere than Belmopan and so Belize City remains the country's commercial capital. By now, the people of Belize City are well accustomed to hurricanes and floods. They enjoy living in their seaport city with its historical associations and its population of some forty thousand, consisting mostly of *mestizos* and black Caribs.

Situated on the Caribbean coast, Belize City is the main port of Belize and, as in most ports, there is always a great deal of activity. Most of the inhabitants live in houses built of wood which are raised above the ground on stilts, as the terrain is swampy and subject to flash flooding. The overall effect of the port, with its shacks and tin-roofed dwellings, is one of untidiness; but the people of Belize City like it that way and, as the city is the centre of commerce, they find plenty to do and many diversions for amusement when work is over.

Belize City is divided into thirteen sections which have names such as Mesopotamia, Queen Charlotte's Town and Cinderella Town. Canals further divide the thirteen sections and, as with many tropical towns which have water running through them,

The canal in Belize City, crossed by the famous Swing Bridge

Belize is notorious for its smelly canals. The reason for this, as visitors soon find out, is that open sewers run right into them. Despite that, Belize City has a quaint air—although many travellers find its general slovenliness, run-down atmosphere and crowded streets none too attractive after the spacious avenues and broad boulevards of Latin American capitals such as Mexico City.

However, Belize City does have a Caribbean atmosphere, and strolling around the streets is the best way to get to know it. Many Belizeans seem to spend a lot of time lolling in the doorways of shops and outside their houses. Two main factors are responsible for this. The first is the intense heat which drains people of energy and makes them listless. The heat inside the tin-roofed dwellings is suffocating. Although the sidewalks may be scorching, even they come as a relief from the infernos within the buildings. The second reason is that drug abuse is a problem in Belize City, just as it is in the coastal cities of Colombia. Because drugs are easy to come by, many of the city's inhabitants smoke marijuana and even stronger drugs which make them incapable of working, and so they spend their time in a world of their own. That is not to say that walking in the city, even after dark, is particularly dangerous. Most Belizeans are courteous and friendly and spend their days working like the people of any of the world's port cities. It is just this small faction that gives Belize City a bad reputation. Although the government attempts from time to time to suppress the drug smugglers, it has had little success so far.

Belizeans passing the time of day. The climate makes the pace of life very slow and creates a very leisurely atmosphere

Belize's chief crop is sugar-cane, and large quantities of rum (which is made from molasses) and *aguardiente* (a sugar-cane brandy) are distilled. This plentiful amount of rum leads to alcohol abuse by a minority of Belizeans. But, on the whole, Belize City is a cheerful place with music blaring from the bars and everyone seeming to be having a good time. The Belizeans believe in working hard and playing hard, and there are many bars with pool tables, fruit machines and ear-shattering music which ranges from reggae to rock and roll.

At the quayside the ships load and unload their cargoes. They arrive from the U.S.A. and Caribbean ports such as Cartagena in Colombia, carrying all manner of goods.

57

A market stall selling produce to the inhabitants of Belize City

Belizeans looking for work often arrive at the port hoping to be taken on as stevedores. Some are lucky, some are not; like many port cities, Belize has its share of unemployment. Drug pedlars also frequent the wharf which adds to the port's general air of sleaziness.

A feature of Belize City is its street markets, the chief one being the City Market. But for those accustomed to the fine display of merchandise seen in other Central American countries, Belize's City Market will be a disappointment. Its fruit and vegetables are a poor sight after the overflowing stalls of mangoes, papayas, guavas, custard apples and other tropical fruits found in the markets of Guatemala and Panama.

The Belizeans were accustomed to imported food for so long that they were slow to develop their own agriculture. Like the

58

port city, the market looks run-down and dirty and the stallholders themselves seem apathetic by comparison with the more flamboyant Guatemalans. For all that, Belizeans still prefer to shop in the market, feeling that the produce is fresher than many of the tired samples in the local food stores. Belize's shops do not have the variety of goods found in other Central American countries, although there is always a display of local handicrafts such as coral, straw hats and tortoiseshell.

The north side of the city is where the best residential areas are situated. Queen Street is the area's main thoroughfare. There, alongside the shops, can be found restaurants, the city police station and the post office. The easternmost side of this

The lighthouse at Fort George

St. John's Anglican Cathedral

district, which is in fact a peninsula reached by the Swing Bridge, was where the eighteenth-century Fort George was situated; it was joined to the mainland in 1922. It is an area much liked by both Belizeans and foreigners, for it includes the Fort George Hotel, one of the best appointed hotels in the country. Northsiders rarely mix with those who loaf about the port. Their homes are often built in British colonial style, with well-kept gardens, full of tropical trees and shrubs.

However, it is the south side of the city which was first developed. Its main streets—Regent Street and Albert Street— were originally called Front Street and Back Street. Slave quarters dating from the nineteenth century can still be seen in these areas. The crowded tenement blocks are now inhabited by Belize City's poor.

60

Belizeans claim that their Anglican cathedral, St John's, built in 1857 and located in the south side area, is the oldest Anglican cathedral in Central America. Further evidence of British rule can be seen at Government House, built in 1814. The British governor still resides here, although today his powers are limited. The Supreme Court, a white-framed building overlooking Central Park, is another excellent example of British colonial architecture.

Of course, life in Belize City was very different in colonial times but, apart from the unavoidable destruction wreaked by floods and hurricanes, the city itself has remained much the same. Although it is a Caribbean port, in many ways Belize City has the air of a British provincial town transplanted to the tropics. In comparison with its Central American neighbours, Belize gives the impression that the British have never left.

The Supreme Court building in Belize City

The Interior and the Coast

Belize's next largest town after Belmopan and Belize City is Orange Walk, which has a population of about eight and a half thousand. Orange Walk lies in the northern part of the country close to the Mexican border. Much of the northern region is given over to sugar-cane growing, and the towns of Orange Walk and the more northerly Corozal, almost at the tip of Belize, are the heart of the sugar-growing region.

Orange Walk, 104 kilometres (65 miles) from Belize City, is the commercial centre of sugar production. It was originally inhabited by the Maya who cultivated crops in the region and built their temples and cities there. Excavations like the one at El Pozito have unearthed some clues as to how the Maya lived in the flat, marshy land which comprises most of Belize. Today, the town of Orange Walk is populated largely by Spanish-speaking *mestizos* whose ancestors originally came from the Yucatan in Mexico.

All around Orange Walk lie wetlands which prove a haven

62

A Jabiru stork in flight

for bird-watchers as all manner of wildfowl can be sighted
there. The marshes and the many lagoons are the home of
storks, egrets and spoonbills, but the patient and enthusiastic
ornithologist may also, if lucky, glimpse the rare Jabiru stork
among the more common herons and waterfowl. Bird-
watching in the Belizean marshlands has become highly
popular and both keen amateurs and professional ornitholo-
gists come to the area, anxious to catch a glimpse of the rarer
species.

Orange Walk controls the sugar-cane production for the
whole of the northern area, and the sugar industry provides
work for many of the inhabitants of the town. Sugar is big
business and the town overflows with cane as it is piled onto

The unsuitably-named Hummingbird Highway, winding its way through the hills from Belmopan to Stann Creek

trucks which take their loads to the sugar refinery. Anyone who has been in, or near, a sugar refinery will be familiar with the sickly aroma which pervades the atmosphere; and in Orange Walk it makes the visitor only too aware that this is indeed a sugar town. Having worked amongst the cane for so long, the workers no longer notice the smell but a first-time visitor senses it immediately.

Not long ago, towns such as Orange Walk and Corozal were difficult to reach due to the treacherous condition of the roads. The journey from Belize City to Corozal, a distance of 150 kilometres (95 miles), once took as long as five hours, but these days the journey takes little more than half that time. This stretch of highway used to be considered one of the worst, if not the worst, in Central America. Riddled with huge potholes, the road was not only hazardous but also extremely uncomfortable, with passengers being jerked from one side to the other of any vehicle. It had a disastrous effect on the vehicles, too; many were severely damaged or broke down completely. Today, four-wheel-drive vehicles negotiate the terrain with ease.

Corozal lies 48 kilometres (30 miles) from Orange Walk in the sweep of Corozal Bay. Corozal is a pretty place, with its palm trees and fine beaches. Here Belizeans can participate in all kinds of water sports. Fishermen, in particular, like Corozal Bay, since all kinds of fish are found there and anglers like nothing better than a good-sized catch. Corozal is also a centre

This railway (shown here during construction in 1911) leads to Stann Creek. When Stann Creek was a centre for banana cultivation, fruit was transported to the coast by train

of sugar production. As in Orange Walk, sugar is the mainstay of the town, providing jobs for much of the population which is chiefly comprised of Spanish-speaking *mestizos*.

Corozal also has the advantage of being close to Mexico, for the frontier is less than sixteen kilometres (ten miles) away. Once across the border, buses transport passengers all over Mexico, on much better roads than are found in Belize, and passes like the Southern Highway (which leads to Punta Gorda) and the Western Highway (leading to Guatemala) make travelling speedier than in former days.

From Belmopan, the Hummingbird Highway leads to Stann Creek (Dangriga) which has a population of about seven thousand—roughly the same as Corozal. Although the Hummingbird Highway sounds as if travelling along it might be speedy, unfortunately this is not the case. Far from skimming over a fine asphalted roadway, travellers are obliged to jolt and bounce their way along the 160 kilometres (100 miles) which lead from Belize City to Stann Creek (Dangriga). Before reaching the busy seaport, those interested in the Maya civilization will notice St Herman's Cave, a series of underground limestone tunnels. Some believe the Maya held religious ceremonies there, but it is more likely that they used the caves as underground hideouts.

Stann Creek, or Dangriga as it is also called, was one of the first European settlements in Belize and dates from the seventeenth century. Black slaves were brought to Belize from the West Indies in the nineteenth century, and every year, on

Musicians like these, playing the marimba, often provide music for people to dance to in the streets

November 19th, the descendants of these black Caribs celebrate their arrival with parades and dancing. Then music explodes in the streets and there is much jollity and laughter. Everyone joins in the celebrations and the music of the *marimba* (a well-known dance rhythm) is heard alongside strident trumpets, singing and dancing.

Boats leave Stann Creek daily for the offshore islands and, like most ports, there is always a great deal of activity. Belize's second port city is the centre for the country's fisheries and citrus fruit production.

67

An Indian village in the Toledo district. Even today the Indians keep very much to themselves

Roughly 130 kilometres (80 miles) south of Stann Creek is Punta Gorda, Belize's most southerly town. Punta Gorda is the chief town of the Toledo district and has a population of about three thousand, consisting of a variety of racial groups including Maya Indians, Creoles, black Caribs and some Chinese, all living peaceably together.

Since the mid-1970s, the Toledo district has been invaded by oil prospectors from all over the world, so nowadays there is an even wider variety of nationalities in Punta Gorda. Literally

68

translated, *Punta Gorda* means "Fat Point"—it is certainly very well named, as the oil prospectors aim to get fat on their profits!

Situated opposite Honduras Bay, Punta Gorda enjoys easy access to Guatemala, and to the offshore islands and cays. Although it has not become the oil boom town many predicted, Punta Gorda's mix of nationalities makes it more lively than it would otherwise have been.

Also in the Toledo district is the Indian village of San Antonio whose inhabitants are mainly descendants of the Maya. This is the one place in Belize where visitors are likely to see colourful local costumes, for the Indians take a pride in their traditional crafts. While much of Belize has a British colonial air, San Antonio offers a picturesque glimpse into the distant past, for it is here that local handicrafts, as well as Indian costumes, are made. Not far from San Antonio lie the Maya ruins of Lubantún. Even though the Toledo district has been thrust into the present by oil prospectors, its historical past is never very far away.

The Maya mountains are situated above Lubantún. Further north, beyond the town of Millionario, lies Mountain Pine Ridge. This is one of Belize's natural beauty spots. The region includes waterfalls, streams and vast pine forests and provides a reminder that, after all, it was the timber forests which brought the logcutters to Belize in the first place. This national forest reserve area is spectacular, not least for its scenic views. In fact, it is Belize's wilderness—a truly untamed area which offers the

69

Hibiscus in flower. This is one of the many beautiful shrubs which are native to Belize, often growing wild

lucky visitor glimpses of genuine wildlife that are rarely seen elsewhere.

The forests are the home of many varieties of wild flowers, and birds, too. The area can be explored on foot or by four-wheel-drive vehicle on dirt roads which lead through the wilderness. This is how Belize must have looked to the early settlers. Waterfalls cascade into valleys, their spray falling mistily into the cavernous depths; and limestone caves bring back memories of the Maya people who once lived there, and their underground hide-outs.

The Western Highway, from Belize City to Guatemala,

passes through the town of San Ignacio which has a population of about five and a half thousand. This is the town to which many of the early logcutters came, and today it constitutes Belize's main logging centre. It is also the hub of the region's cattle-raising industry. San Ignacio has changed little over the years and preserves a tough attitude to life, recalling the days of the early logcutters, who had a hard existence in Belize's forests, hewing down timber to send back to Britain.

The highway leads on to the Maya ruins of Xunantunich on the Guatemalan border. Close by is Benque Viejo with its population of about two thousand. This is the westernmost town in Belize and, like the people of San Ignacio, its Spanish-

The border crossing into Guatemala

speaking citizens are a hardy breed. They are descended from Guatemalans who came to Belize to find work. Links are still maintained with Guatemala. Benque Viejo is often dubbed "the smugglers' town", for much contraband passes between it and Guatemala. Perhaps this is not surprising, considering that Benque Viejo is only a short distance from the frontier. Benque Viejo maintains the picturesque lifestyle of Guatemalan towns and villages; nonetheless, the present-day inhabitants consider themselves to be Belizeans.

Islands and Cays

Belize's beaches of white coral sand provide a spectacular contrast to the country's steamy mangrove swamps and pine forests. The islands and cays off the coast are among the finest in Central America. The majority of the cays are uninhabited and their very remoteness makes each one seem like a faraway tropical paradise. Robinson Crusoe and Man Friday would have been happy to make their home on them, for the sea is crystal clear, the sands are white, the fishing is superb and the peace and tranquillity make them seem worlds away from the teeming capital cities of Latin America.

The Turneffe Islands, almost directly opposite Belize City, are the largest of Belize's atolls or coral islands. They comprise several islands extending over 777 square kilometres (more than 300 square miles), and are criss-crossed by passages through mangrove swamps. On the Turneffe Islands the visitor gets the true feel of Caribbean atolls. The water is beautifully clear, enabling the keen coral reef diver to see many forms of aquatic life. As for fishermen, the Turneffe Islands present them with a challenge, for these waters are well supplied with tarpon and bonefish. However, it is the permit fish which presents the biggest incentive, for this swift and powerful specimen, although plentiful all year round, is no easy catch to land. When a fisherman comes home with this highly prized trophy, he can feel justly proud. Amberjack and kingfish are both plentiful and, for both divers and anglers, Belize's Coral Barrier Reef is an exhilarating place to be.

Thirty-two kilometres (twenty miles) off the Turneffe Islands lies Glover Reef. Its most developed area is Long Cay at its eastern end—a popular spot for divers, anglers and water-

An aerial view of one of Belize's many cays. This one is an extension to the barrier reef, which stretches across the picture

Yachts belonging to foreign visitors moored at Ambergris Cay

sport enthusiasts. Glover Reef is a truly tropical isle where the pressures of city life do not intrude. Its coral formations and underwater life are a paradise for the naturalist and scuba diver. In the past, coral has been ruthlessly hacked from many Caribbean seabeds with the result that black coral, which grows to a depth of 95 metres (300 feet), is now a great rarity. Most divers, however, mindful of the hazards of indiscriminate plunderings on the coral reefs, are now trying to impress on people the importance of bringing up only a small amount— otherwise the coral beds will soon be stripped completely. Due to the scarcity, coral now fetches high prices in the market. It is a good thing that people are becoming increasingly aware that, as coral takes many years to grow, they should appreciate the splendours of the underwater world and try to preserve it.

75

**A sandy street typical
of San Pedro**

Ambergris Cay lies 56 kilometres (35 miles) to the north of Belize City and can easily be reached by air or sea. Ambergris is the biggest of all the cays and the best known — probably due to the fact that more people visit it because it has an airstrip. Its chief town is San Pedro, where the sandy streets give the sensation of a truly remote and sleepy Caribbean atoll — a complete contrast to life in the big cities.

The islanders are carefree and cheerful. They are only too ready to down tools and play the guitar or any other musical instrument to hand, for they love the haunting rhythms of the Caribbean. If they are not singing and dancing, they are swopping fishermen's yarns, for San Pedro is a true fishing community.

Most of the inhabitants of Ambergris Cay earn their living from fishing. They developed the Caribbean Fishermen's Co-operative so that they could pool their resources and fish for shellfish such as lobsters and conch. These days they have a thriving industry, exporting conch and other shellfish to the U.S.A. As the fishing industry of Ambergris Cay developed, the islanders became self-sufficient. Confident that the fisheries will continue to make them prosperous, they are happy-go-lucky people. Visitors to Ambergris Cay remark on the relaxed atmosphere, despite the fact that that these days Ambergris Cay is getting more than its fair share of visitors. Hotels have been built on the cay so that people of all nationalities are coming to dive, snorkel and fish.

Immediately south of Ambergris Cay lie Cay Caulker and Cay Chapel. As on Ambergris Cay, most of the six hundred inhabitants of Cay Caulker are involved in the fishing industry. After the development of the Northern Fishermen's Co-operative, their catches of fish brought them prosperity. Like the fishermen of Ambergris Cay, those of Cay Caulker feel secure and content, knowing that the fishing business will support them.

There is no air service to Cay Caulker but there is a regular boat service from Belize City. The islanders like it that way, for

Hotels built on Ambergris Cay to house water-sports enthusiasts

they can preserve their community without being overrun by tourists. All the same, they are not averse to foreigners and are only too glad to assist them and show them round the cay.

As on Ambergris Cay, the streets of Cay Caulker are sandy and completely unpaved. There are no four-wheeled vehicles on Cay Caulker, and the islanders have maintained their old traditions without too many changes.

It may seem surprising that a small islet like St George's Cay, a mere sixteen kilometres (ten miles) from Belize City, was Belize's capital from 1650 to 1784. It was off St George's Cay that the sea battle of 1798 was fought, when the Belizeans defeated the Spaniards. Today their victory is celebrated as a holiday on September 10th each year, and is known as National Day.

The early European woodcutters settled on St George's Cay, exploiting the mahogany forests of the island. The Cay was used as a hide-out for pirates and buccaneers who looted passing ships carrying cargo to and from Europe.

In the entrance to Belize City harbour lies English Cay. It has a lighthouse which is responsible for guiding ships into the harbour. English Cay is a coral reef greatly loved by Belizeans for they can picnic on the sands at weekends in the shade of palm trees. Swimming and water sports are excellent on English Cay.

Half Moon Cay, 112 kilometres (70 miles) off the Belizean coast, has a lighthouse too. This lighthouse was built in 1848 to guide the cargo ships carrying their precious loads of timber

A boat taxi transporting people between islands which lie close to each other off the Belizean coast

from Belize City to Europe. Lighthouses were vitally important, for the dangerous coral reefs could easily damage the ships, causing them to sink. Added to that, there was the increasing fear of pirate attacks in Caribbean waters, for the buccaneers of the coves and bays were ruthless. Many ships never reached their destination, their precious cargoes being off-loaded instead into the pirates' hide-outs.

The waters off Half Moon Cay are reckoned to be amongst the finest in the world for divers, and visibility is good to a depth of over 60 metres (200 feet). All kinds of fish and coral, and even underwater stalactite formations, can be seen.

For those who prefer to stay above the water, the beaches of Half Moon Cay are superb, their white coral sand contrasting sharply with the aquamarine ocean. To the south of the cay lies a bird sanctuary where many species of birds, some indigenous to the Caribbean, can be seen.

On Half Moon Cay itself is a large transparent lake in the centre of which is situated the Blue Hole, an underwater shaft with a drop of 122 metres (over 400 feet). The Blue Hole contains a variety of underwater stalactite formations and is thus of interest to divers and oceanographers. It is an area of mystery and, like Loch Ness in Scotland, there are many stories of unknown creatures lurking in its depths. Some people claim to have seen blue-eyed monsters or strange reptile-like creatures but no one knows for sure if any such creature exists. It may be that divers who see the Blue Hole as a challenge to their diving skills secretly hope they will see something out of the ordinary!

80

Some of the cays are mere specks on the horizon, but for many visitors the offshore islands remain one of Belize's greatest assets. They are among the few semi-isolated places that remain on the earth's surface. How long such idyllic retreats can remain unspoiled is a question for the conservationists. In the meantime, life on most of the smaller coral islands goes on as it has done for centuries. Ambergris Cay and the Turneffe Islands have their holiday camps and hotels, but as yet the tourist business has not made much of an impression on these still remote atolls. Tourism is likely to remain limited and this means that for some time to come the coral reefs can be assured of peace and tranquillity.

Belize Today

Although Belize is a Central American country, it is, nevertheless, very different from its neighbours, all of which have Spanish as their main language. The official language of Belize is English, and evidence of British influence, following the many years of British rule, is still strong.

Although Belize was granted independence from Britain in 1981, it remains part of the Commonwealth with a British governor and British army, navy and air force units to protect its frontiers.

Britain is ready to give Belize total independence, but the people themselves have unanimously voted to remain within the Commonwealth. They feel that, if they had complete independence, Guatemala might persist in its claims to the country and take over without consulting the people. Despite the treaty of 1859, when Guatemala was forced to accept the British presence in Belize, Guatemala has systematically refused to give up its claims. Every so often, the old arguments

Banana cultivation. The fruit is encased in a treated bag to encourage growth and to keep off insects

flare up again. With the discovery of oil in Belize in the 1970s, Guatemala began to take an even keener interest in the country. If subsequent oil strikes prove profitable, it may be that not only Guatemala but other countries as well may try to get a foothold in Belize.

There is no doubt that if Belize were economically stronger everything would be different. But poor living standards and the lack of any major industry make it difficult for the economy to develop.

Belize has to rely on agriculture, with sugar as its most important crop. Efforts are now being made to make Belize less dependent on sugar by introducing other crops. Although Belize suffers from a lack of skilled workers, the country has

Harvesting sugar-cane, Belize's most important crop. The work is extremely hard in such a humid climate

been carefully divided in order to make the best possible agricultural use of the land. The northern sector concentrates on sugar production, while in the south citrus fruits are cultivated. Recently cattle-raising has expanded and the planting of ricefields should also give the economy a boost. As Belize does not have the great variety of fruits and vegetables enjoyed by its Central American neighbours, it was decided to start market gardening to provide produce for use at home as well as for export to the U.S.A.

Belize's Caribbean coast is the home of several different varieties of fish, so Belize's fisheries could also be developed. The islands and cays, particularly Ambergris Cay and Cay Caulker—where the Caribbean Fishermen's Co-operative and the Northern Fishermen's Co-operative are based—are doing good business exporting lobsters, conch and other shellfish to the U.S.A.

Although at the present time industry in Belize is limited, some small-scale industries are proving that success will come in the long run. New incentives and projects are being proposed and, with the necessary cash loans from other countries, Belize's industry should be able to expand. The population is small but that does not mean that new schemes cannot be tested. Construction is one area in which Belize could certainly expand and, although the workforce cannot compete with those of larger countries like Guatemala, Belize is eager to develop in this field.

Belize is a member of CARICOM, the Caribbean Common Market, and trades not only with its Central American and Caribbean partners but with other nations as well. It is still dependent upon imports from Britain, West Germany, Japan and the U.S.A., but at least the Belizeans know they cannot go on relying on imports as they have done in the past. The economy cannot be expected to improve overnight, but within the next few years Belizeans should begin to see a gradual change for the better.

One of the major obstacles to improving the economy is the

A secondary school. Expenditure on construction of public buildings is evidence of Belize's growing economy

limited transportation system. Roads are still poor in Belize, although they have improved quite dramatically in recent years. However, heavy rains often wash away some of the roads during the wet season, making access impossible. Better roads are essential if Belize is to transport the goods it produces and compete with its Central American neighbours. No one is willing to go on jolting over potholed roads, which make journeys not only extremely uncomfortable but also lengthy, when they could ride along paved highways.

This is one reason why tourism has never developed in Belize and why the country is still considered to be "off the beaten track". In one way this works in Belize's favour, for while a country remains remote and different it has something unique to offer. Belize's terrain may be flat and swampy, and its climate hot and humid, but the country does possess one of the most spectacular coral reefs anywhere in the world. The many islands and cays are a delight for sailors, fishermen and divers, and the famous Blue Hole on Half Moon Cay has attracted some of the world's most renowned oceanographers. Belize is also a paradise for bird-watchers who come in search of the rare Jabiru stork. Archaeologists are attracted by the number of Maya ruins to be found in Belize, while other people come to explore the wilderness with its immense variety of flora and fauna.

Much has changed since the far-off days when the European settlers' chief occupation was cutting down the timber forests, sending the mahogany, rosewood and cedarwood back to England to be fashioned into furniture by such masters as Hepplewhite and Chippendale.

With the first oil strikes in the 1970s, prospectors began to move into Belize, and oil-drilling began both on and off shore. The Toledo district was besieged by speculators and two foreign oil companies moved in. It became a common sight to see oil-men from all over the world strolling through the town of Punta Gorda, side by side with the ethnic mix of people already living in the region.

In a sense, oil-prospecting opened up new horizons for Belize. People began to hear about it in news reports all around the world, while oil-speculators grew optimistic about major

The present-day face of part of Belize City, in contrast with the older buildings and poorer areas

strikes. Although no significant strikes have been made as yet, it is to be hoped that the further development of its oilfields will one day put the small Central American country of Belize firmly on the map.

Index

92